Burn

PAUL VERMEERSCH

MISFIT

ECW PRESS

CANADIAN CATALOGUING IN PUBLICATION DATA

Vermeersch, Paul
Burn

ISBN 1-55022-436-0

I. Title.

PS8593.E74B87 2000   C811'.6   C00-931725-2
PR9199.3.V47B87 2000

A misFit book edited by Michael Holmes
Cover and text design by Tania Craan
Author photo by Andrej Kopac
Layout by Mary Bowness
Printed by Veilleux Impression à Demande Inc.

Distributed in Canada by General Distribution Services,
325 Humber Blvd., Toronto, Ontario M9W 7C3

Published by ECW PRESS
2120 Queen Street East, Suite 200,
Toronto, Ontario, M4E IE2
ecwpress.com

The publication of *Burn* has been generously
supported by The Canada Council, the Ontario Arts Council,
and the Government of Canada through the Book Publishing
Industry Development Program. Canadá

CONTENTS

PART TWO

days without hearing a sound

the days dogs die

If you don't get a good night kiss,
you get Kafka dreams.
—BILL WATTERSON,
CALVIN AND HOBBES

BOOLARANDAH

My father puts his shovel down and holds me
over a deep hole in the lawn. He tells me
a monster lives in this hole and her name
        is Boolarandah.

An eight-legged frog, an albino alligator
with cloudy eyes like the dog next door.
My father laughs and wiggles me like bait.

I throw a toy soldier and his parachute opens.
He falls through centuries deeper than oceans;
slowly and peacefully he floats beyond the fence
        to safety in the uncut grass.

When I Was Superhuman

Once, I wore Lake Huron for a cape.
A chunk of driftwood was a ship
I could capsize with a flick
of my wrist and watch
my enemies drowning inside.

Bursting from a wave,
flecked with black and rotten leaves
and the abandoned husks of young
mosquitoes, I blocked out the sun
and stormed crazily through villages of sand,
exacting my revenge.

I was a powerful, beautiful boy,
and I could call down thunder and lightning,
      you know,
            if I really wanted to.

THE DAYS DOGS DIE

The days dogs die are usually good days
for barbecues, nice sunny days, perfect
for eating watermelon and dangling
your feet over the sides of things,

those days the asphalt gets a little
sticky from the heat, and voices
carry clearly down the avenue,
kids you don't know the names of —

one girl you caught wasps with last summer.
Pretty one, what was her name again? Erin?
You set a jar full of yellow jackets in the sun
thinking they were bees, that they'd make honey,

but instead you both watched as they fell
lifeless to the bottom, turning black,
the day her father's green Reliant swerved
by the park gates at dusk, and your miniature

poodle a shadow in the shadow of the car.
It took six of your sister's friends to hold you
down on the porch, to keep you from running
to the road, to see the carcass, or even to save her —

whatever it was you were trying to do.

Rural Elementary

Jamie Lyle was playing circus by the turkey crates,
tightrope walking, holding a mop handle for balance
when he fell into a vat of liquid manure and drowned,
so Mr. Palmer the principal called Father Borghese
to come to our school and tell us why we die,
and reassure us that Jamie had been baptized
and wasn't going to Hell.

Kevin Vranic was lucky; Kevin tumbled
off the back of his dad's tractor, lost an arm
and missed the rest of grade three.
When he came back he had to get up on stage
to talk about his accident, and the whole school
gathered round to watch Kevin pick up a pencil,
opening and closing the hook on his new arm
by flexing a muscle in his shoulder.

He had to take it off to play soccer; that hook
could hurt someone, rip someone's shorts, poke
someone's eye out, and Scott Hague and Dave Skinner
got suspended for throwing the arm into a tree,
but Kevin climbed to the top and got it down —
all by himself.

A Portrait Of My Sister's Roommate

The girls all threw their arms around me
at the funeral, couldn't stand on their own
with Michelle's cancer
spreading through them by way of grief,

                               and after
her mother gave the eight-by-ten,
the one displayed above the guest book,
to my parents
            for being generous enough
to have the wake in their own house.

They thanked her for it,
placed it on the television set
so all the guests could see,
                and later,
when the deviled eggs were gone and paper plates
filled four green garbage bags,
                  and everyone
was finally gone, they put it in the basement
with my grandmother's knick-knacks,
my paintings from high school,
and all the other things
they never wanted in the first place,
                    but keep.

THE SKAGGS BOYS

Ronald Skaggs had a neck like an arm,
long and bent, an elbow for an Adam's apple —
everyone called him The Ostrich.

And people said Sam wasn't born retarded —
he was normal til the summer he turned eight.

We all thought Geoffrey would end up
in jail. His hard skin made up for the bones
in his wrists, which were always slung in casts.

And the legend went that Ryan got burned
when his father got angry and drenched him
with hot grease, but he didn't have any scars
that I could see.

The four of them lived like picks and shovels
in the dirt. They were blamed for everything —
for the egging on devil's night, bloody lips,
for stolen bicycles, missing cats,

the things we had to live with.

We Saw The Ocean Together,
We Were Young

I imagine a boy genius who could lift sixteen ton
trapezoidal weights over his head and shoot red lasers
from his eyes, and he is hilarious; his tongue hops
in his mouth like a frog in a jar. But really
he was short and blonde and shifty-eyed, and everything
he said was a joke:

> *So the husband says:*
> *Who's the cheap bastard*
> *who gave you twenty-five cents?*
> *and the wife says:*
> *Everybody.*

Nathan showed his teeth
a lot. We weren't exactly friends, but
we saw the ocean together, we were young.
It's a shame really. Only fifteen. A normal boy.

The moments that had to be pieced together
by the evidence, I've imagined a thousand times —
the footsteps on the stairs,
the musty smell of the basement. Nathan
alone.

The motions he went through,
like taking his own
photograph:

Point the camera at yourself.

Show your teeth.

Click.

WILDWOOD DRIVE

Boys, four of them, thumping the dirt with ape shouts,
chasing a girl into the trees, and they say the Earth
has changed more in the last one hundred years
than in a hundred thousand. The girl looks familiar.
Large pale fish-blue eyes that narrow so tight
they could snap toothpicks, bones, but she's afraid.
The ground here has been hollowed out
to build a church. Fat mounds of local dirt
veil the trees from the neighbourhood,
and no one can see them
but me.

They've got her by the pantleg, and they're pulling,
but she continues to rise, up into the leaves, until
she's out of reach and naked from the waist down, crying,
Gimme my pants back! C'mon guys, her voice broken,
losing its humanness, *Gimme my pants back!*

What they see is a girl with eyes bulging, her ears
turning red, twitching, thick hair starting to grow
all over her body, a tail. They roar
with laughter, pick up sticks and pound the trunk
until the leaves are shaken loose.

A sudden gust of wind blows dirt in my eyes
and they water a little, but I remain still. As leaves
are torn from the tree, the girl's arms and legs
are tied in a bow around the trunk, and the boys

throw their sticks at her, but their sticks blow away
in the wind.

No one can see them but me, hiding behind a ball of clay,
wondering when I'll have the courage to pounce
these blockheads and teach them a lesson, like Hercules,
King Arthur, Bugs Bunny, my heroes, but they
were all bigger and stronger than me. Inspired, however,
by the thought of The Crusher pinned to the mat,
I emerge from my hiding place and yell, *Hey!*
Why don't you guys just leave her alone and
give'er her stupid pants back.

And wind is wrenching dirt off the hills in clumps now.
I'm being pelted by tiny stones, fist-sized
tufts of sod, and fists. Blood pours from my mouth,
my lips, I think, and all the wind
has been knocked out of me as the boys kneel
on my arms and chest and insert long, sharp blades
of crabgrass into my nostrils until I scream, my voice
broken, losing its humanness, and from the corner of my eye
I see the girl dropping to the ground and running
home, with her T-shirt pulled down to her knees.

THE BURNING BOY

Whenever the punch came from behind,
Mike's fist was the catalytic flint,
knuckles scraping the scalp, sulphur
and black powder dyed red, fantasizing

                a slow turn,
the back of my head bit-by-bit becoming my face,
becoming wood, a special effect designed to terrify and

*(as though a hand had come down holding a match to
set me on fire)*

              flames beginning at the point of impact,
in my hair,
then spreading to ears, nose and throat, across the shoulders,
tongues running down bare arms, little blue flames popping
up from the skin, the gas on now, the heat building
when the chest goes, then torso, groin and legs
become engulfed, just like that, and
                        I am the burning boy,

*(faster faster the wanton flames grow rapid make me twice
maybe*
three times my size)

                impervious to heat, ablaze and stepping
across the playground, visible from the air in rolling flames
and sickly trail of smoke while panicky classmates
cry and run and watch me, laughing,
                      but still that ache

where the punch landed, angry and wanting
to reach out, on fire,
                    grapple my attacker, hold him
in my burning arms, roast him, incinerate him,
make him holler, thinking of the yellow squeeze
bottle of Ronsonol lighter fluid hidden in my dresser,
even if I just filled it with plain water, even just
to scare him. No match for his strength, it's the only way
I can hurt him.
                    Because I can't hurt him.

THINGS LIKE THIS HAPPEN EVERYDAY

All three of them I guess were lying on the front lawn,
on the grass, and drivers coming down the tenth line
could see the mom, dad and teenage son, stretched out

in the late spring warmth, eyes locked on small clouds
drifting across blue heaven and the dark silhouettes of
tree branches wavering at the edge of the property.

The grass being damp started soaking through their clothes.
Tips of thousands of blades of grass brushed their finger tips,
their palms, their wrists, the backs of their necks, their hair.

Mother, father and teenage son, a family of three were lying
on the grass in front of their farm house on the tenth line where
passing drivers could see them stretched out in the midday warmth.

They weren't lying in a circle or triangle or with their feet
all pointed together in the middle, they weren't holding hands,
but lying wherever they happened to fall, no real design to it,

and after quite a great deal of time several sets of tires skidded to a halt
on the nearby gravel driveway and some people got out and they began
shouting instructions to each other, and one man had a megaphone.

A Minor Gothic Incident Near The End Of The 20th Century

My mother called out my name,
                              terrified. *Hurry,*
come quick. So holding a towel
around my waist with one hand and dripping
                              shampoo and water
all over the carpet and the shower
still running, I said
                              — *what's the matter?*
but her fear was a skeleton
that could not be articulated.

It seems young Robin Redbreast,
with fine new feathers and poor guidance,
had got himself stuck in a stack of chairs,
and,
        hanged by the neck,
was staring at her through the patio doors.

Do something do something,
                              she screamed, so I ran
to the garage
                for the gardening gloves, and
having lost my towel somewhere
in the vicinity of the kitchen,
                              went out,
in full sight of neighbours, onto the deck
and rescued the damn bird, carefully
supporting its head and body in clumsily

gloved hands,
                    and I held it
in my lap by the fireplace where it finally
shit on me
                    and died.

There were tears,
                    which I blamed on the soap
in my eyes, and when I buried the bird I buried it
the equivalent of six feet down, at least,
in the relative measure of birds.

SCENE FROM BRIGHTS GROVE ONTARIO DURING THE REAGAN ERA

The pink rubber skipping rope
left on the driveway in sunlight
will crumble,
            and the trees will leave
shadows, Lake Huron will evaporate, and my sister
in the kitchen, hysterical, positive
she's just seen a soviet warhead
flying over Crabbie's 9 Hole Golf Course,
not six blocks away.
                    She knows from school
the plants in nearby Chemical Valley,
Dow, Dupont, Imperial Oil,
are among the top ten targets in North America
after Washington, New York and someplace
in Texas . . .

My mother
singing,

    It's probably just an airplane, honey,
    there's nothing to worry about,
    honey, it's okay

trying desperately to calm my sister,
and convince herself.

Shadowing The Medivac

He's already in the car, an hour's drive
he can't allow himself to think, just drive
in the helicopter's shadow peeling

silently over the hills, silently, like nothing
is happening inside, nothing going on,
can't think of anything newborn

zooming through the sky, an ounce of brain
racked by seizures, blue-skinned, underweight
and Swiss cheese for a heart.

What's in the rearview, eh? Anything coming?
Cars? Trucks? Glare and a crab-red face deformed
with thoughts of beats and breathing tubes,

and ahead, old magazines on tables, waiting rooms
where doctors lead men and women into offices to sob
oh my god oh god oh jesus no . . .

And some of the most beautiful scenery in this country
can be found along our many well maintained highways.
Shield rock, tamarack swamp and pine groves

line the winding thoroughfares between our cities. He is still
driving, he can see the city coming up. The helicopter
must have arrived already, in Toronto, where they fiddle

inside her rib cage with the sanitary version of a bicycle tire repair kit . . . and he's on his way to the hospital, he'll get there, he's coming, he's keeping his eye on the road.

FISH TALE

Sometimes just knowing a person
makes your arms ache
for an embrace. Like fighting a salmon
desperate to shake free,
you put your whole back into it,
and the line breaks, and the boat rocks
long afterwards.

The way she tells it: she was twelve
on the riverbank, said she went
looking for crayfish to keep in a bucket,
then boys came along,
to her, inside her, bringing her
thinly rolled joints, contraband powders,
serums, and junk to ply her
open and steal her heart
chamber by chamber,

> and now she's floated away,
> to Vancouver, with god
> knows how many hooks in her.

OCCASIONS FOR WHISPERING

we drink gin we hear her confession
secrets to keep from the next room

she sleeps she dreams her scars fall away
turn into bumblebees the Disney kind

she is so sorry a mighty tear rolls off her cheek
it hits the ground like a glass piano

a little woman in long white gloves
plays a fugue the whole way down

I hold her in my arms I say
I know I know I know . . .

and there are two sunsets now the second one
has heroes riding into it

she is so breakable instantly like a grasshopper
she leaps from a cliff but does not grow wings

THE BIRTHDAY PARTY

No one's going to finish their cake
until she comes out of her bedroom
and stops crying. You knew

she didn't like cherry filling
but really you just bought the cake
that you wanted, didn't you?

Well, someone's got to clean up
the pile of torn wrapping paper on the
dining room carpet. Someone's

got to get the stain out
of the seafoam green chenille sweater
she got from Eatons, but

do you think you can ever
take back what you said about her
being a freak and a queer

and a dyke? The neighbours
excused themselves with a great deal
of class, I think.

THE SEARCH PARTY

Locals started to gather in the parking lot
of Waterworks United Church and newcomers
tripped over yards of yellow police tape

wrapped from post to tree as flashlights
sliced their bat-blind pathways cross the field.
All the cops in orange vests directed
volunteers to line up at arm's length
and to keep in step during the routine sweep,
til Fred McNealy told the lieutenant

her seafoam green chenille sweater
was found bogged down in the heavy wet grass
near the lip of the Cow Creek ravine.

days without hearing a sound

What will become of you and me
(This is the school in which we learn . . .)
Besides the photo and the memory?
(. . . That time is the fire in which we burn.)
— Delmore Schwartz
"Calmly We Walk through
This April's Day"

PLAYING HEARTS
December 1998

At the table my mother wants to know if Hearts
have been broken.
             Someone answers
Yes. She throws the queen down. That's her trick.
I'm safe.
           Who wants another beer? I ask,
heading for the garage. *Dad?*
                    Yeah sure, he says.

             Later I will reach
over the coffee table, grab the toe of his slipper
and give it a shake. *Dad, go to bed*, I'll say,
you're snoring.

             He will open his eyes slowly,
look at the news and close his eyes again,
fall back to sleep, and this will happen maybe
two or three more times before he finally gives up
and goes to bed.

Then I will sit by myself in the decorated living room,
where it is impossible to crack walnuts after midnight
without waking my niece. The volume is turned
all the way down. I'm reading lips. Fred is giving
Wilma a bowling ball for their anniversary. Oh Fred.

Tomorrow night is Christmas Eve, another game
of Hearts . . . people will ask if they've been broken.

Yes, someone will say, *they have.*

Last year for Christmas I got a new coffee maker
the year before that, a new duffle bag and some
good blank notebooks, before that it was paints
and I don't know, I could keep going: Nirvana albums,
action figures, water guns, until . . .

I am being carried into the house from the car,
still sleeping.
        If I was awake I'd assume the snow
flying around my house is also falling on the pyramids
in Egypt, somewhere a crocodile is lying on a bank
with a little pile of snow accumulating on his head,
between his eye-bumps.

My cousins come over a little later in the afternoon,
on Christmas day about seventeen years ago. Then,
when their car pulls out of the driveway to head home,
I run to the window to wave goodbye, and I find
their triceratops wedged between the sofa cushions.
Oh no, we have to stop them, I say,
                              but it's too late.
My parents accuse me of hiding it there, accuse me
of stealing the dinosaur.

I knew it was wrong.
I did it anyway.

Falling asleep in the decorated living room. The whoosh
of the natural gas fireplace is not enough to disturb me.
It's your deal, Paul. Someone says. The game is on.
And you want to know if Hearts have been broken.

THE SLOW DEATH OF HIS MOTHER'S MOTHER, EUNICE, QUEEN OF EGYPT

First one leg, then the other,
amputated below then above
the knees, seems her whole
life was like that,
buried one piece at a time,

including her husband —
he is passed out on the couch
for all eternity, deep beneath the plot
where the entire house of their married years
has been buried deep,
for good.

Visiting her grandchildren
at Christmas, she wasn't held
like a dog coming home from the vet,
or carried in like a new lamp.
No, she stayed in her chair,
like Cleopatra on the
shoulders of loyal servants,
and she came floating
through the front door
smiling and brushing
the delicate snow from her lap.

Sea World

I

this house is nothing like the jumping of dolphins

She never wants to leave
the house, she never wants
to leave, the woman who lives
in the house on the hill.

The living room has new furniture
and murky underwater light
when the shades are drawn —

bulrushes could grow in mid-air,
god, the rings that interlock
on the coffee table from glasses of wine
have multiplied and become
so finely mottled and lacy, so
darkly textured and tropical,
it seems the wood must have grown that way,
that it must have been very expensive.

The woman has fallen
asleep on the couch, toys
litter the carpet; a boy shoots coyotes
in the backyard with a bb gun
while lounging on a boulder
by the swimming pool.

This house, this house

on the hill, is nothing
like a fun-filled afternoon
at Sea World, San Diego.

II

that which swims forever to the left

It's Tuesday and the crowds
aren't so bad. The woman who fell
asleep on the couch woke up
and drove us here.

We can't believe she left the house,
but here we are at Sea World,
and all I really want is a killer whale
to come out of the water and kiss my face,
like on TV, but I was crushed
when they chose the other kid,
the kid from the backyard wishing
he had his bb gun
so he could shove it down
the whale's blowhole
and pop it one.

They should have chosen me;
I've always believed
that if a wild animal touched me,
I would gain its powers —

if a whale touched me, I would be able
to swim like one, leap from the water,
and dive deep with built-in sonar.
If I touched a gorilla, I'd be stronger
than ten strongmen. I could fly
if I was wearing a coat
made of birds.

There is a petting tank, though.
I am feeding minnows
to a pilot whale. It is smooth,
hairless and amazing black,
and I'm smooth, hairless
and red with sun.

Holy communion, tossing minnows
through a mouth the size of an oven door,
but Jesus Christ the whale lunges
and I swear I feel teeth.

Stunned and dizzy, overcome by the strange
whiteness of everything, the white sun
and all of San Diego, I sit down
on a box of geraniums, to catch my breath
and count my fingers.
There are ten.
Good.

III

a three hour flight, a day at the beach

I look the whale in the eye, show him my hand,
show him I'm okay, and we understand each other,
how we both got here, how we both ended up
at Sea World. The whale knows all about
Air Canada flight 083, about the little
bottles of Coke, the skin on the tapioca,
the house on the hill, the van coming over here.
And I know this:

    here is the sole survivor of a pod that beached itself
    on a golf course in South Carolina. The golfers
    dumped their clubs on the sand and dragged
    gallons of seawater up the beach in their golf bags
    to moisten the skin of the stranded cows.

    For thirty-six hours they worked with biologists
    and rescue volunteers, cursing the poor things
    for beaching themselves at hightide, and cursing
    their smooth dark skin for absorbing the sun.
    Finally eleven whales were returned to sea.

    They swam out to the mouth of the bay, and then
    turned back, including this one, a calf,
    looking for its mother (they say a whale in the North Atlantic
    can hear another whale's song as far away as Cape Town),
    and the rest were slowly crushed to death
    under the weight of their own bodies.

IV
agoraphobia/claustrophobia

The woman who fell asleep on the couch
is drinking something weak
beside a cage of Andean condors.
They have heads the size of pears
and ten-foot wingspans.

She senses the open miles around her
impending like water
on the riveted seams of a submarine
or escaping like air from the lungs
of someone sucked through the blown hatch
of an orbiting spacecraft.

There must be twenty thousand people here.

The condors flap their wings,
their genetic memory.
They have a different understanding
of endless space, how everything hovers
just above South America
trailing over the plains and jungles
to the East, where the birds are bright blue
and eat fruit, and over the ocean
to the West, where the birds are white
and eat fish.

To the woman who fell asleep on the couch
endless space

is anything larger than a living room.

There must be twenty thousand people here.
There *must* be a way
to be like them.

THE HOURS
for my father

Lucky to be alive. The Austin Mini
left the road with surprising frequency
come to think of it, surviving the S curve
on Lakeshore,
              going 55 before the days of metric.

If you felt invincible then it was probably your
bride-to-be (then equipment manager) or some other
you haven't mentioned since, or that yellow acoustic guitar
in the passenger seat coming home from rehearsal . . .

                              (Your kids found it
down in the basement, played with it until the strings
disappeared, don't even know where it is now.)

              Favourite movie: *The Graduate*

Remember the feel of football pants? Tight yet forgiving.
Hidden pockets stuffed with turtle shells, bulked up the skinny,
trimmed the fat, and those square-top Frankenstein helmets over
square-top Frankenstein haircuts.
                              Hey?
Remember Bryl Cream?
(Didn't mom brush her teeth with it once?)
                              Kept playing
football even after you changed schools, former teammates
yelling, *Get him! Get that Percy!*   Mom says it was the only time
you ever scored a touchdown.

No hair on your legs below the knees from spending summers
wading in tobacco gum, you learnt to smoke and stole raw stuff
from the boss, you and John S., a couple of kids,

                                        and that first car
you drove out to the back of the field, killed the fuckin shocks
busting one foot furrows of clay. Couldn't take it home like that
so you left it there, til weeds grew in the seat stuffing and things
started living in it.

                    It's dirt now.

And where the hell did that guitar go? Did you give it to somebody
with Tom and Jerry dreams of the big time? Legendary, just like
The Kingston Trio. Remember the songs?

  Where Have All the Flowers Gone?
  Remember the Alamo?
  Hang Down Your Head, Tom Dooley.

Ed Sullivan's introduction, you could almost hear it:

  Ladies and gentlemen,

    The Hours!

 Hey,

   what ever happened to those guys?

BLACKBIRDS APPEAR

Everything that happens
around my grandmother's house
is temporary. Red-winged
　　　blackbirds appear
and disappear on the wire fence.
Their entire lives,
a thought of rain-fat night,
scattered seeds, a moment just,
then wind blows
them out like candles.
　　　For a few hours
yesterday white sheets
were hung outside to dry.
　　　The dog next door
barked all night
for years, then stopped.
　　　People, children,
grandchildren. Come, leave, summer,
autumn. The lights go out
in one room, go on in another.
　　　There was a man here
once, quiet as dust
lying in places you never look.
　　　They had brought their children
here and watched them leave
and come and leave and red-winged
　　　blackbirds appear
and disappear on the wire fence
　　　in this place

where it is almost always early morning,
           and the rain
      is always just starting to stop,
and a person, say,
      my grandmother,
           can go days without hearing a sound.

The Migration of The Buffalo

There's something you should know before you read this poem:
Belgians, when they settled in Southwestern Ontario
after World War Two, were nicknamed "Buffalo."

I

The M.S. Georgic

My father's family crossed the Atlantic
in a ship with a lofty name
rusty windows, and the smell
of mildew, bilge and galley fare —
farewell rabbit stew, farewell endives,
farewell Tante, Noncle, farewell
exploding fields of cabbage,
farewell good chocolate. Hello
new world, to each man an acre, hello,
       hello, hello.
The night he couldn't sleep, he went
on deck, and the only dry land in sight
was the dead, white face of the moon.

II
The Little Pick-up Truck

With all their belongings
loaded on that little truck,
they must have looked
like the Beverly Hillbillies,
or like the Keystone Kops
when the truck bounced
out of control across that field,
and the box got stuck
between two trees,
and the cab just kept on rolling.

But they made it anyway,
to Lambton County, somehow
like home with all these stones
with names like Vogel, Vandenheuvel
and Vermeersch,
                    these buffalo.

Joseph, The Carpenter

My grandfather, with a set of hammers
all scarred from use, and with sweat
pushed through his grey crew-cut
with walnut fingers, built lives
for his children.
    Hell, he could build
anything if he had enough wood,
even a whole tree with odds and ends
from his workshop, even make it grow
leaves.
    Damn, he was a good
carpenter; he could drive big nails flush
in one swing, and with the same hands he used
to raise my dad.

THE UGLIEST TREES I'VE EVER SEEN
West Flanders, visiting the dying relatives

They were ugly, polled,
all their branches cut,
but new branches would grow
from the stumps, come spring,
my father told me,

and those branches, the ones
that had been cut, they fuel
the fires that cook the stew,
hold up the roofs of houses.

But still, these trees were
like cancer patients, you know . . .
you really hate to see them like that,
all shaved and thin.

West Flanders Farm House, 1986

Aunt Julia had a lump
in her breast that showed
through her apron,
but it wasn't an issue.
She stormed around
the kitchen, hands full.

At thirteen I couldn't help
staring. That lump.
But the other children

just dipped sugar cubes
in their coffee, quietly
sucked the sweet liquid,
let it crumble in their mouths.

THE VIRGIN OF THE BOMBSHELL

The Virgin Mary appeared to me in the basement
hundreds of times when I was a kid, in a hollowed out
bombshell, a grotto of iron lined with red velvet.
She stood bearing a crowned heart, a tongue of fire,
flanked by two brass 60 millimetre machine gun rounds
bolted on either side, herald angels of the war's end.

Some Flemish farmer risked his life to carve that hole,
not knowing if the shell was live, spent all of one franc
on a plastic figurine of The Mother of God and maybe
ten francs on the velvet — an act of Catholic voodoo
to protect his house from bombs.

It had belonged to my grandmother. God knows
where she found it. We sold it in a garage sale
when I was still young enough to climb trees and carry knives,
and still it sits on a shelf in the carefully labeled vault
of my childhood, my museum.

Behind it, on its shelf, is the Last Supper
done in paint-by-numbers by my grandmother,
which we kept in the root cellar after she died.

At The Godsfield Clinic

Sure as Hell the lawns are nice,
beautiful lawns, green, manicured,
lush, trim, damn fine lawns, and

all around the main entrance
they've planted queen's fire
violet explosion and black parrots.

In the lobby there's a fountain
with goldfish, some of them
big suckers, swimming through hyacinth

and a good half-inch of tarnished coins
in a soapy film at the bottom.

In a common room a woman is talking
to a man whose head is half caved-in,
part of his skull removed, and

down the hall another woman sits
at an easel in the arts and crafts area
staring through the doorway, thinking.

I don't know where I am,
or who these people are.

A man in room 75 is wearing
a clean, pressed shirt. His hair is cut
short and combed neatly to one side.

A blue-green bauble worn at the throat,
like cheap plastic jewellery for kids,
breathes for him, cycles his air

through a hose into a metal box
        with gauges and dials.

He still has partial use of his arms
and his thumbs have become long
and distended like the other fingers

that don't obey him anymore, but
he can still adjust his eyeglasses
wipe his nose, tap short messages

on a keypad, like a man
from the future, they say, when we
won't need our bodies anymore.

His daughter was here this morning
with his grandson, six months old,
but she had to go to work.

Another man, in long johns, lies crippled
on another bed and mutters to himself.

Three years of this. Three years.
       Three years of this.

Outside the window tanned young men
are starting lawnmowers. Their sound
fills the hallways of the clinic.

The bed rails rattle as they pass by,
and blue smoke cuts across the garden.
They might take the whole afternoon.

MARIGOLDS AND PEONIES

When everyone worried about
filling their cars with gasoline,
a young boy was often taken
to kneel upon brown grass,
say prayers and contemplate the dead
withered heads of marigolds,
his grandmother's favourites,
which look too much like dandelions,
his own mother says, and which crumble
on their stems, leaving burnt yellow flakes
everywhere around the stone, like confetti.

Years later, when gasoline was abundant
and grass was green, his father felt the plot
needed a little something, so he planted
peonies, because they come back every year,
unlike his son, and at least that's better than nothing.

ONE MORE TIME WITH JOE
False Memories Of My Grandfather

I

Hoisting me like a hurdy-gurdy
monkey to his shoulders,
one hand lifting me into place,
Joe holding my ankles tight
like straps across his chest.
Together we almost make
a tall man.
                    Wherever it is he takes me
there is something, a new colt,
an old car, there is something he wants
to show me.

II

That time we walked, it was Victoria Day,
to the marina, all of us, to watch the fireworks,
Joe stood next to a sailboat called
"One More Time" beneath galaxies bursting in green
flames, and the bay smelled like dead fish
and gun powder.
                With every boom the crowd
gathered on the other side of the hill
Ooooooed and cheered while Joe thought
of the startling destruction of happy farms long ago,
and he messed up my hair with his fingers
and opened a beer for my dad.

III

Even though the farm often smelled
like pigshit, I will never forget the day
Grampa Joe stepped onto the porch,
and I followed him,

watched him through the screen door
as he tried to smell the whole world
all at once, drawing healthy lungfuls
of country air and lighting up a cheap
White Owl cigar, and his head jerked,
noticing something. He said, *Look at that,*
would ya look at that, that's beautiful.

I don't know what. I wish I knew.

In This Land I Could Dig

In this land I could dig and find the dead
a few feet down and find
the dark soil where one has died
and a little deeper where the bones
were put on a Sunday.

A full scale excavation will reveal
bombs, bullets, and broken pacemakers,
and farther down the dead
among the shoes and digging tools,
the eyeglasses and rags,
gold watches and bone-handled spoons,
and farther down the dead,

enough to elect their own government,
so close they could all join hands.

those days you could still speak my name

And it's a sadness what they've done to the women I've loved:
they turned Julie into her own mother, and Ruthe —
and Ruthe I understand has been turned
into a sadness . . .
— DENIS JOHNSON
"OUR SADNESS"

Melanie Panhandling

                    outside the Rex Hotel
five years ago, probably August the heat was so bad,
just turned 18 and shaved her whole head bald,

except for the braided rattail with rainbow elastics
that hung down like a prince's lock between
her shoulder blades, her breasts, she was trying

to get enough together to get to Fredericton
for a cousin's wedding.
                    My father won't drive me, she says
cuz he's an asshole.

                    Anyway . . .

                    Dagwood,
her one year old Rottweiler, is sleeping in the sun
behind her; he's all muscle and having a nightmare —
he whimpers and kicks at the wall in his slumber.

Melanie's arms are bare, her hands are ready
to receive coins, rain, her tongue uncurls
like it might catch a snowflake, the way

                    lions yawn in the sun

and there's a stainless steel ball punched into her taste buds
like a pearl in an oyster you love the way it slides down
your throat.

Did it hurt? I ask.

Only one guy, she grins.

I laugh and Dagwood stirs, lifts his head and growls
at me, so I decide it's time to go.

For blocks I can think
of nothing but Melanie's tongue, its clean wet sphere,
its purpose. I told myself I'd forget about her,

but I don't know about that.

MEGAN ON FERNWOOD AVENUE

They Might Be Giants in concert,
Ann Arbor, Michigan. I met Megan
when I was seventeen.

Me on the balcony,
her on the floor below
daring me to spit
into her open mouth,

and because she looked
like a young Darryl Hannah,
only dirtier, I told her:

Come upstairs, so
I can get a better shot.

We exchanged letters
for years — she wrote
drool drool drool
on the envelopes —

the sex life
of an American girl:

Dear Paul,

I sucked off this skinhead guy
named Mike last week at a party
in the bathroom. He told me

he wants to marry me, but
I don't know if I should . . .

Dear Paul,

That Mike guy is history.
He said I have to quit smoking
or he won't marry me. Well
screw that! No one can make me
quit smoking, not him, not my mom,
not anybody . . .

Dear Paul,

I tried speed for the first time
last night, and oh my god, it's
such a rush. I ended up in bed
with this black guy named
Angus. I just had to write and tell you . . .

Dear Paul,

Larry wants me to have an
abortion, but I don't know, like,
what if I'm killing the next Einstein
or something . . .

Dear Paul,

Hey, I heard from someone
who knows Mike that Mike
got killed in a knife fight
over a sandwich or

something like that.
I guess that's too bad,
even though the guy
was a total dick. Still,
it's kinda weird knowing
that someone you fucked
is dead . . .

I don't know when
the letters stopped —
probably when she got
old enough,

or too old.

ALONE IN THE BATHROOM
HE REMOVED HIS SHIRT

God how he admired the scarecrow and Jesus
on the cross, sunken gut and ribs you can count.
Alone in the bathroom he removed his shirt,

neatly folding it over the back of the toilet
he examined himself, sucked it in, he only stood
on the scales when he was naked and dry.

His belly ached empty. One monastic bowl
of porridge every three days, that was it.
For lunch he'd bike sixty kilometres,

then drink a glass of water, you need to have water.
He stayed home from school, lied about nausea,
lounged by the pool in Bermuda shorts getting a tan,

somehow thinking the sun would shrink him faster,
as near as possible to vanishing, but not quite.
In time the pangs inside became a tingle,

like after coming. He grew thin and cried for joy
the day he punched a new hole in his belt.
He turned in front of the mirror half the day

becoming a small white flower, becoming almost
seventeen years old, as the ribs began to emerge
like cypress roots in a barren season. He craved

to count them all and find one missing.

THE PERFECT GUY FOR L

In her bedroom L is wearing a white V-neck T-shirt, which,
on her, is casual and pretty the way it drapes over her
and clings to her body,
                              and we have become friends,
both single, so we bitch
about how we can't find anyone,

but L declares the perfect guy for her is
dead anyway, so why bother?
                              Remember I was telling you
about Jeff Buckley?

                              She picks up a picture
cut from a magazine and framed in a small ornamental
heart made of silver,
                              telling me: *Look how his head*
is thrown back and look how good he looks
in that white V-neck T-shirt, so plain so
simple. See how it clings to his body?

                              L explains
his mysterious death, drowned in an off-shoot of the Mississippi
near Memphis; no one knows how.
                              He'd waded out into
the water, still in his clothes, singing
as the gentle wake of a passing boat began
slapping the breakwater. His friend only
turned his back for a moment,
to move the radio, and when

he turned around again

                    the river was just the river.
He'd only slipped in all the way to get his hair wet, maybe.

Maybe opening his eyes he saw the Sun as a trace
of flickering Zippo warmth, a will-o'-the-wisp
flitting above his head, and he wished for it
to land on his outstretched fingers, humming
something buoyant and soothing

L plays his album for me and says
his death was such a shame because
she would have married him, truly, yes, she would have,
                            on and on,
                                      He was so
gorgeous, just look at him, guitar, white T-shirt,
those lips, those . . .

Her voice trembles a little and she looks away from me.

Maybe for L, he'll always be there,
in her blind spot, like glare from the sun
when you're underwater, humming something
buoyant and soothing, throwing his head back and singing
grace and hallelujah.

                        And L turns up the volume
so we can hear everything
and not feel the need
to speak anymore,

her bedroom suddenly dim as the sun moves behind a building.

Rare Aphrodisiac

Someday, darling,

                  all the tigers will be dead and gone

and the sun-dried pricks of our perfect killing machines,
salted and stored
              in candy jars
at the Chinese pharmacy,
                  will be worth millions

        but Christ,
               how they killed
                          on the banks of the Mekong,
bright leaves come alive to rip out the antelope's throat, oh
how they rolled out
the low growls
              and blood soaked roars

and savagely fucked by the river at dawn.

                        Perhaps this occurred to me
because there was a picture of a tiger
at the party where we met,
                 awash in pink martinis,

        and the night,

as we stepped into it,
            kissing,

was purely mammalian, darling,
the temperature of blood,
and for days I could still see the purple
teeth marks you left in my shoulder.
They were my proof.
At least I had proof.

Still,
    I can't pinpoint exactly when it occurred to me,
but it did occur to me —
when the young men in white shirts
finally bag the last tiger,
when the wily beast rears up
against the levelling of rifles,
and the jungle stands still
pretending not to notice,

when the sad bastard
rumbles the last word for his kind,
a spiteful cry
that will go unrecorded,
when the triggers are squeezed
and the poor thing jitters into oblivion, biting
at the pain before the end, biting the slick holes
flamed into his coat,
as the young men watch the last tiger

violently try to escape his own brain, the killing brain
in paroxysms, at the last, at the end,

before they finally skin him, slice out

that long thin cock for a fortune,

it occurred to me —
                    when that happens,
the moment the tiger falls, that you might be beside me,
somewhere, consoling me
for some other,
                    unrelated sadness:

    a dying friend, a bad prognosis, an accident,

                                    something horrible,
and you would be the mate to my unhappiness,

but I'm sorry, darling, no, I can't
                              remember exactly

        when that might have occurred to me.

Concerning The Events
Of October Fifteenth

You had to get up and dance all over the place
just to keep from freezing, and I sat still,
so what I saw, and what you didn't see,
        was a meteor

in the east; it made a small incision
between two stars in the bear's belly, just beyond
the cars heading nowhere at 1 a.m.,
        and the wound opened

just like that, with you shaking underneath it,
and then it closed again . . . zip . . . gone.
I really didn't think it was worth mentioning.
        I didn't think

that maybe Jupiter driving by in a blue Mercedes,
checking his hair in the mirror, driving forever,
flicked his cigarette out the window and
        (while you were cold and shivered)

I watched it spark across the wet streets of heaven.

LAPSE

Yes, yes, of course, I passed twenty-two
windmills on the way to your house,
a half-hour out of the city,
hay fields rolled up and tied for fall,
broken barns, dead dogs and chopped trees,
new ones each year.

The new black tights, red plaid skirt,
and dark grey sweater you wore that day
we went shopping in London, the day
my mother said you were beautiful, yes . . .
like it was yesterday.

And the night we sat in front of your house
on the grass beside your oak tree, yes,
but not the way your palms felt
against my back, for the life of me,
those days you could still speak my name.

GIRLFRIEND AFTER BREAST REDUCTION SURGERY

*there is nothing at all I can do except hold your hand
and not go away*
— Al Purdy, from "Poem"

I

All day in the hospital with her mother,
sweet jesus he's dying
for a smoke,
                but she doesn't know, of course,
she doesn't know he smokes;
she still thinks he's a good influence
                                on her daughter.

There's a pack of disgusting Indonesian fags
in his pocket —
                they smell like cloves, incense,
baking ham,
                like smoking potpourri and dirt
rolled in dried banana skins.
                        They're horrible,
but the filters taste like candy,
                        so he likes them.

                He never used to smoke
and now he needs a fix like he needs food and water,
                no,
like he needs to escape from a trunk,
                but he doesn't dare excuse himself

and come back smelling like that,

so he waits,
and his limbs all strain with an awful craving
he hides like a scar beneath his watch.

II

Finally, they roll his girl out of surgery,
groggy,
        down the hall on a gurney.

Don't touch her —
              body like wet plaster
              needs to gel right, set properly.

From halfway down the hall they can already see
she's awake,
        in a way.

Her first words: *Do they look smaller?*
It's all she can manage.

Under the gauze she's wearing a surgical bra
to keep things in place:
              mammary glands, draining tubes,
              at least four inches of padding.

She's got a morphine drip with her own hand-held control.

I better get home now, her mother says, *get supper started,
or no one's gonna eat tonight.*

He offers to walk her mother to the car,
now that she knows everything's gonna be okay.

No please don't go, whispers the girl

in a fog of painkillers,
please don't go, she whispers —

but not to her mother.

III

When her mother's gone
he lingers in the parking lot,
smokes a cigarette.

        The tremors subside.

Look man, he says aloud to himself,
you gotta get a grip on this.

It's December but the snow hasn't stayed.
The lawns have all been frozen, thawed, flooded,
fucked-up and frozen again —
footprints and wheel ruts frozen

                solid as the sidewalks.

Nothing ever stays nice, he says. He's twenty.
Black sweater and blue jeans. No coat.

Nurses huddle on the hospital steps
with steaming coffee and cigarettes.

This is serious shit, he says, blowing smoke. The wind
is all over him. The hospital is big and old.

Feels like someone punched him in the gut.

Her scars are gonna be noticeable.
She's gonna lose sensitivity in her nipples,
probably.

During the operation
                    they cut
     her nipples out
                    like the little faces
  you cut from magazines,
        then put them back on,
  glueing the little faces on different bodies,
                              higher up
               on smaller bodies,
so they'll be in the right place
                    when she's done.

He wonders what the doctors do
with all the stuff they remove.

He tucks one hand under an armpit and finishes
his smoke,
          flicks the glowing end away, watches it
roll around in the street
                    til it burns out,

and then he smokes another before he goes inside.

IV

Back upstairs his cheeks are red.
I thought you were gone, she says.
I was afraid you weren't coming back.
You smell good.
You smell like an old boat, she says,
but it might be the morphine talking.

She was supposed to have a private room,
but they put her in with two old women
with Crohn's disease.

The crones with Crohn's, she drones.
They yammer on about bedpans,
how quickly they fill.
One tries to make it to the toilet on her own,
but doesn't quite make it across the room.

They make obscene noises, they belch.
They are visited by dozens of loved ones.
They have hyperactive grandchildren,
and one has a husband who sings
and plays harmonica.

The other one gossips about people
the first one never met.

Tell them to be quiet, she begs. *I need sleep.*

Okay, okay, he says, but he's afraid to move the curtain.

He doesn't want to be there. He hates it there. He hates it.
He wants to leave, he really wants to, but
there is nothing at all he can do except hold her hand
and not go away.

Idea For A Film

I'm thinking a feature length documentary called

The Cleaning Lady

because the girl who cleans the toilets
in the building where I work
seems young enough
that maybe she's working
her way through school,
taking night classes in accounting,
or maybe something computer related,
so that one day she won't
clean toilets anymore.

The cameras will follow her from her apartment,
a fall day with her hair still wet when she steps out
and pulls the door shut behind her. They will get on the bus
and go to work with her, film a day in her life,
not just the cleaning, but they'll get close-ups of the rings
on her fingers, in her earlobes, the cover of the book
she's reading.

Stainless steel.
Gold.
Of Mice and Men.

She'll visit all eighteen floors. On one floor everyone
will know her name and invite her to join them
for a donut. On another floor no one will speak to her,
and she won't say anything but, *Is anyone in there?*

She has long, naturally curly red hair, freckles
and green eyes. Her name is Jennifer,
or Sarah, or Rachel.
She misses her old friends. Her mother
is proud she's doing so well.

Rainstorm

The sky is so fat, it hangs low
over the bright grove.

Oh look here comes the rain
you say, and it comes
warm and heavy off the lake,
wide skyloads of light flicker
and boom.

You go hop-skipping through a puddle,
and I chase after you because

sometimes when you look at me
I notice a slow ghost moving through the room,

wearing your perfume, touching
my back.

You And Me And The Toronto Transit Commission

Maybe you didn't notice, but I Gene-Kelleyed down the stairs
    into the station behind you, and I
don't usually dance. The organ of courage
was inflating inside me and it felt like someone breathing
    on the sex lobe of my brain.
The dial on the safe in my chest was turning
    right sixteen, left twenty-five, right again thirty,
and the heavy titanium-reinforced door was swinging
    open to reveal a hundred pairs of eyes
glowing in the dark. Maybe you didn't notice,

but as we stood together on the platform, beautiful
white moths swarmed over the fluorescent lights above us
    and made everything flicker, like you and I
were in an old movie about me and you, and we were
playing ourselves, and everyone else in the world
    was an extra, just there for the day.
Maybe you didn't see the tiniest gum wrappers floating
    on air-cushions, alive for a second
before the train slammed past us and screamed to a halt
    just inches from our bodies,
like being narrowly missed by lightning.

The Cook Comes Home For Love

Muscles and bones all useless
at the end of the day, and I stink,
wearing a skin of olive oil
and flour, the food
a hundred other people eat.
I shed my clothes at her front door,
and tell her I need better shoes,
something more comfortable,
and she, dressed for bed
at the kitchen table,
says there're leftovers
in the fridge. I step naked
into the steaming bathroom
to scrape away my work
with the sharp edge
of a thin blade of soap.
I put on a clean shirt
and eat from her bowl
so there is only one dish
to wash before we sleep.

The Narrow Bed

knees inside the crook of hers,
a problem with arms that sleep solves,

but I wake and she's on the floor,
smoking a cigarette lit
in total silence. On the floor,
by the window, she is
something shaped by streetlights,
the occasional moon,
and the pennies we scattered
in gentle fumbling the day
before yesterday,
and sitting on them,
breathing smoke, she is
the beginnings of a dragon,

invincible but hunted to exhaustion.

She swore she couldn't sleep facing me,
*We'd breathe each other's breath
and suffocate*, she said.

THE DAY I DIDN'T HAVE ANY FUN
for David McGimpsey, I guess

I had a girlfriend once who took me
to her family reunion in a church hall
in the middle of corn fields and nowhere.

I think they knew someone was going to die
because even second cousins were there,
and one of them had a baby with a rare disease

that only affects one in two million newborns —
a large sac of fluid hanging from her neck
and everyone said she was beautiful.

I learned twenty names in five minutes
and worried I'd be ostracized if I didn't remember
all of them. We had roast beef and potatoes.

I couldn't figure out if these people
always ate roast beef and potatoes, or
if they never ate roast beef and potatoes,

because everyone said how much they loved
the potatoes, and have you ever tasted
potatoes this good in your entire life?

And I thought what's so great about
the god-damned potatoes? They're just a side dish.
They're good but they're nothing special.

*What about the beef? Don't you people care
about the beef?*

FOR A YOUNG WOMAN WHO COMPLAINS THAT MEN KEEP FALLING IN LOVE WITH HER

You must think they all want to be beautiful
young heroes who walk on the moon.
They all have that floating step, don't they?
Almost weightless with their empty pockets
and they've all heard the reports:
how great brave men have already made
giant leaps at the crater's edge,
how no wind or rain will ever disturb
the footprints they've made there,
and how the rocks they brought you are precious
— but dull.
       Well,
             I'll never make it
to our own particular moon, but look,
these rocks in my pocket I found on the beach:

this one glitters, and this one's light purple,
and I think this green one's a piece of broken glass.

Union
for Peter

It wasn't a white dress
and tuxedo affair. No.
She was in red
like the kind of morning sky
that warns of bad weather,
and he was all dapper and businesslike,
but with a flower pinned to his left lapel.

After the ceremony they drank their fill
and danced like hell, but
that's all over now.

What You Wish Wasn't True

The night you lost it forever,
the night you were supposed to be
at the movies, that night

snow covered the basement
windows, and no one saw in or out
the night the two of you

got closer, attention torn
from the fuzzy sitcom to each other,
you were all hands and

she was all surface, you
were taking the big step, she pulled
the afghan tighter

around you, she'd been
saying for months that when it happened
it had to be perfect,

that night

a kid you knew from school,
you'd seen him around, talked to him,
he snuck into his uncle's

cellar, unhooked the burly
stock of the old shotgun from the rack,
gave the devil

head, and made it come,
and you had to tell the grief counsellors
next day at school

Go screw yourselves, and
you blubbered for a whole half hour
in the upstairs can, seems

manhood was proving
to be a little much, and a year later
remembering, reliving

that night, she confessed
you weren't really the first.

12 Days Waiting For The Mail

DAY ONE   I've been told it will happen,
but when will it happen? My hands,
my blankets, are getting cold.
Fall will be here soon, and the fair
is only for a couple of weeks.

DAY TWO   I went to the fair and all the chickens
had their beaks clipped to thin yellow
holes. I was wearing that cream-coloured
sweater, and the smell of the animal barn,
darling, hurry, before it's gone.

DAY THREE   There was only going to be one letter
I wanted to open today, but
it didn't arrive. It would have been
the one with the fabulous foreign stamps:
the fish, the palace, the brilliant dead youth.

DAY FOUR   The first time I saw her might
have been the fall of 1975, though
I can't be sure. I was young myself.

DAY FIVE   If you think the walls are white
and the floor is bare — you're wrong.
There's a sofa bed, a little table
with a drawer. The walls are lemon,
you know, and I've been taking it easy,
thinking of a comedy.

DAY SIX   A guy at work swears that years ago
in Naga Town, Cebu Province, Philippines,
he drank fermented coconut sap called "tuba,"
looked into the bottom of his glass
and saw the back of his own head.

DAY SEVEN   What if I leave the house today
and see that young woman
break down sobbing
in the restaurant again?

DAY EIGHT   Not what I wanted, but a postcard
from a friend in South America
with canaries on it anyway.
Do you know the canaries' song?
Here is a translation:

> *We are canaries yellow, and we*
> *are yellow canaries, we are*
> *yellow, yellow, yellow. Never*
> *ask us any more than that.*

DAY NINE   Telling secrets to strangers is a booming trend,
like: I'm in love with someone because
I hate her laugh, and we've all said,
I shouldn't even be telling you this.

DAY TEN   Six times six is thirty-six, Mercury
is the closest planet to the sun, and her
long brown hair will pass my window
this afternoon, but she won't see me
watering my poor geranium.

DAY ELEVEN   No one can change the fact
              that she refused to kiss me
              goodbye at the elevator
              because someone nearby
              might see us.

DAY TWELVE   I've been thinking about turning
              on a light, about making something
              to eat, maybe
              banana-something,
              about how today is Sunday,
              and no one delivers the mail
              on Sundays.

INTERRUPTION

Whatever the weapons were in his dreams:
baseball bats, butcher knives or boot heels —
they gave him the night-sweats pretty bad.

He'd kick off the covers and strip
nude in the dark, but suddenly cool,
his body evaporating into the room.

He rubbed his belly in soft circles,
cupped himself and wondered what he'd give
to have someone there when he rolled over.

Muddle-headed in the deep, can't hold on
to thoughts; they slip away, mutate, become
wall-shadow dementia, being watched.

In time, the swirl of air from his nostrils
will make his body cold. He'll pull
the blankets up to his neck again,

turn foetal and drift back to sleep.
In the morning he'll brush his teeth,
spit in the sink, look himself in the eye.

He'll stay like that for a while, fixated,
like a nervous dog growling at the fence —
confrontational and full of contempt.

Burn

Meanwhile near the opposite pole an albatross
wings along one of the Earth's great circles,
winter, and the heavens are resounding purple,

and elsewhere a festival continues to rage
on Queen Street.   Inside, someone is speaking
into a microphone. Comets move

through our system. The BamBoo is dark.
A woman squints for me in the doorway,
joins me at my table. She tries to tell me,
          Hello.

It will be cold everywhere soon,
even underground, and the reports of birds
trapped inside will rise, believe me.

The comets Shoemaker-Levy
and Hale-Bopp dogfight
somewhere below the belt of Orion;

the former returning to score the swirled
smoke hide of the planet Jupiter, a skip-stone
leaving horrible scars on the pond.

These are the facts: the festival, yes,
the woman stirs her drink, Jupiter is injured,
and the albatross crashing the surface,

the sudden cold and the caught fish
giving itself up to death, saying, *This
is my body. This is my body.*

Tomorrow morning will still be cold for most of us.
Some of our foreheads will burn, and none of us
would ever dream of leaving our beds,

not like this — not unless something changes.

Acknowledgements

The author would like to acknowledge the financial support of the Ontario Arts Council.

Some of the poems in this book have previously appeared, often in slightly different versions, in the following publications: *The Antigonish Review*, *The Canadian Journal Of Contemporary Literary Stuff*, *Descant*, *dig*, *The Fiddlehead*, *The Gaspereau Review*, *The Instant Anthology*, *The Lazy Writer*, *The Literary Review of Canada*, *The New Quarterly*, *Pottersfield Portfolio*, *Queen Street Quarterly*, *Taddle Creek*, and *Word*. Thanks to all the editors responsible. Thanks, particularly, to John Degen and *Ink Magazine* for being the first.

The poems *Birthday Party*, *Melanie Panhandling*, *The Perfect Guy For L*, *Shadowing The Medivac*, *Rural Elementary*, *Wildwood Drive*, *Alone In The Bathroom He Removed His Shirt*, *What You Wish Wasn't True*, and *The Search Party* were published in a limited edition chapbook called *What You Wish Wasn't True* from Wayward Armadillo Press in 1999. Thanks to jennifer LoveGrove, the publisher of Wayward Armadillo, for her friendship and support.

The poem *The Skaggs Boys* was published as a broadside by above/ground press.

Enormous thanks to my trusty Sherpa, misFit editor Michael Holmes, for taking this book on and seeing it through. "Here's to all the Futures!" Thanks also to Jack David, my publisher, and all the staff at ECW Press.

Heartfelt thanks to the late Al Purdy for granting me permission to quote from and paraphrase his "Poem" in "Girlfriend After Breast Reduction Surgery," and also for his generous advice. May his poems be read for generations to come.

Special thanks to my dear friend Peter Darbyshire, who was the first audience for most of these poems, for his steadfast and longstanding friendship, for his support, for his editorial comments, for putting up with a lot of crap from me, and for the occasional loan. Thanks, man.

Special thanks also to Jonathan Bennett, a true friend and gentleman, for holding open all the doors, and also to Wendy Morgan, for all the gin and tonics. And thanks again to J.B., along with good buddy George Murray, for a trusty (and last minute) proofread.

Several people read the manuscript in various stages of development and made comments. I thank them all, especially Gordon Johnston, who was instrumental in preparing the manuscript for submission.

The support and encouragement of the following people and establishments has meant an awful lot to me while writing this book: Janet Inksetter and Annex Books; Stan Rogal and Manny at The Idler Pub; Kevin, Winston and Mason at The I.V. Lounge; Allan Briesmaster and the Art

Bar Reading Series; Carleton Wilson and Writuals; The Fantastic Four; the gang at Book City; and Sheila Heti.

Thanks to Sherwin Tjia for the wonderful painting on the cover.

This book is dedicated to my parents Percy and Carol Vermeersch, and to my sisters Shelley Mickalko and Jodi Gordon, with love. I thank them for their love and support and for the stories which inspired many of these poems.